I0644141

Understanding Copyright

Suzy Rabbat and
John Willis

DIGITAL CITIZENSHIP

LIGHTBOX
openlightbox.com

LIGHTBOX

Go to **www.openlightbox.com** and enter this book's unique code.

ACCESS CODE

LBXL2684

Lightbox is an all-inclusive digital solution for the teaching and learning of curriculum topics in an original, groundbreaking way. Lightbox is based on National Curriculum Standards.

LIGHTBOX SUPPLEMENTARY RESOURCES

SHARE Share titles within your Learning Management System (LMS) or Library Circulation System

CURRICULUM Find national and state curriculum correlations

CITATION Create bibliographical references following the Chicago Manual of Style

STANDARD FEATURES OF LIGHTBOX

AUDIO High-quality narration using text-to-speech system

ACTIVITIES Printable PDFs that can be emailed and graded

SLIDESHOWS Pictorial overviews of key concepts

VIDEOS Embedded high-definition video clips

WEBLINKS Curated links to external, child-safe resources

TRANSPARENCIES Step-by-step layering of maps, diagrams, charts, and timelines

INTERACTIVE MAPS Interactive maps and aerial satellite imagery

QUIZZES Ten multiple-choice questions that are automatically graded and emailed for teacher assessment

KEY WORDS Matching key concepts to their definitions

This title is part of our Lightbox digital subscription

Lightbox Grades 3–5 Subscription
ISBN 978-1-5105-5424-5

Access hundreds of Lightbox titles with our digital subscription. Sign up for a **FREE** subscription trial at **www.openlightbox.com/trial**

Understanding Copyright

Contents

2 Lightbox Access Code

4 CHAPTER ONE
All Kinds of Property

10 CHAPTER TWO
What Is Copyright?

14 CHAPTER THREE
Smart Steps to Using Information

18 CHAPTER FOUR
Giving Credit

22 Quiz

23 Key Words/Index

1 Chapter One

All Kinds of Property

The book you are looking at now is someone's **property**. It may belong to your school library. That makes it the school's property. Maybe you borrowed it from the public library. In that case, the public library owns the book. It is the library's property.

Video games are just one of many types of intellectual property.

What are some things that belong to you? Your video games, books, and clothes are all examples. These are your property. They are all things that you can see and touch. But there is another kind of property.

The first time the term "**intellectual property**" was used in the United States was during the **19th century**.

Nate loves playing video games. One of the games he owns is called *Amazing Soccer*. A video game designer named Jenny Smith developed this game. Jenny designed how *Amazing Soccer* would look. She also decided how Nate and other kids would play soccer with the game. Jenny Smith was the creator of the **intellectual property**. Her thoughts and ideas were used to create the game.

In **2010**, intellectual-property-based businesses **added more than $5 trillion** to the **U.S. economy**.

The owner of a book's intellectual property may be its writer, or it may be the company that published it.

If you have ever written a song, you have created intellectual property.

The word "**intellect**" has to do with a person's mind. It refers to someone's thoughts or ideas. When a person writes a song, the words and melody are created by the songwriter. The songwriter is the creator of this intellectual property. A drawing is an artist's intellectual property. The artist is the one who imagined the drawing and then sketched it.

Try This

Who owns the intellectual property for this book? You will find the answer on page 24.

History of U.S. Copyright

1787
The U.S. Constitution states that Congress should protect the right of authors to own their work.

1870
The Library of Congress is placed in charge of **copyright** administration.

1897
Congress declares that the U.S. Copyright Office is its own unique government department.

1988
The United States joins the Berne Convention, working with 24 other countries to protect copyright.

1992
Congress adjusts the law to make copyright renewal automatic.

1998
U.S. copyright terms are changed to life plus 70 years.

2021
On January 1, works written in 1925, including books by F. Scott Fitzgerald and Virginia Woolf, become public domain in the United States.

Mapping Copyright

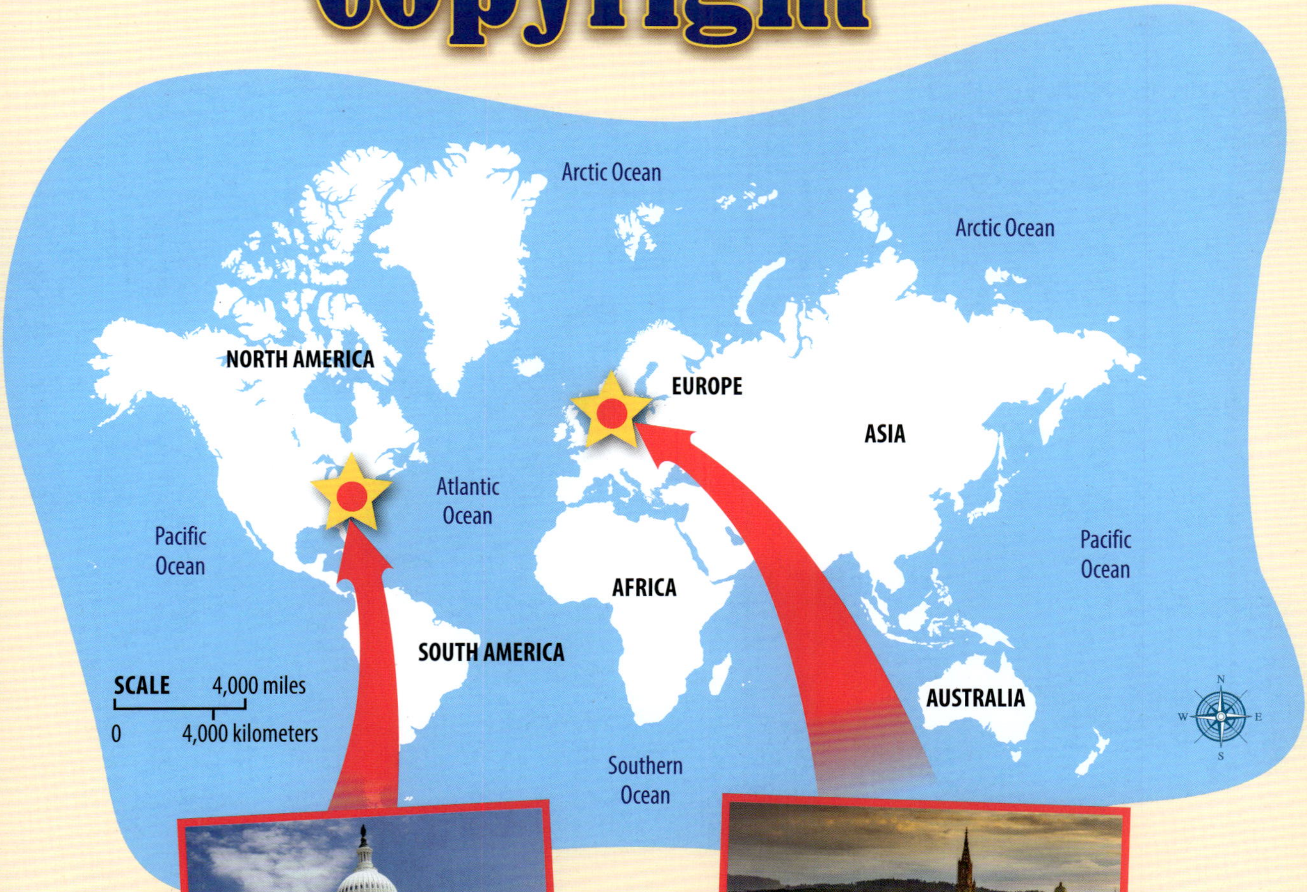

Washington, DC, 2019
The U.S. Copyright Office registers more than 547,000 different works.

Berne, Switzerland, 1886
The Berne Convention is adopted by 10 countries to protect intellectual property. Today, 179 countries have joined it.

2 Chapter Two

What Is Copyright?

Nate's friend Mike lives down the block. Mike just got a new bike. He left the bike on his driveway when he went inside for lunch. Nate would love to try out Mike's new bike. Would this be a good time to borrow it? Mike is not using it. Nate could get it back before Mike finishes his lunch.

A person's bike is his or her property.

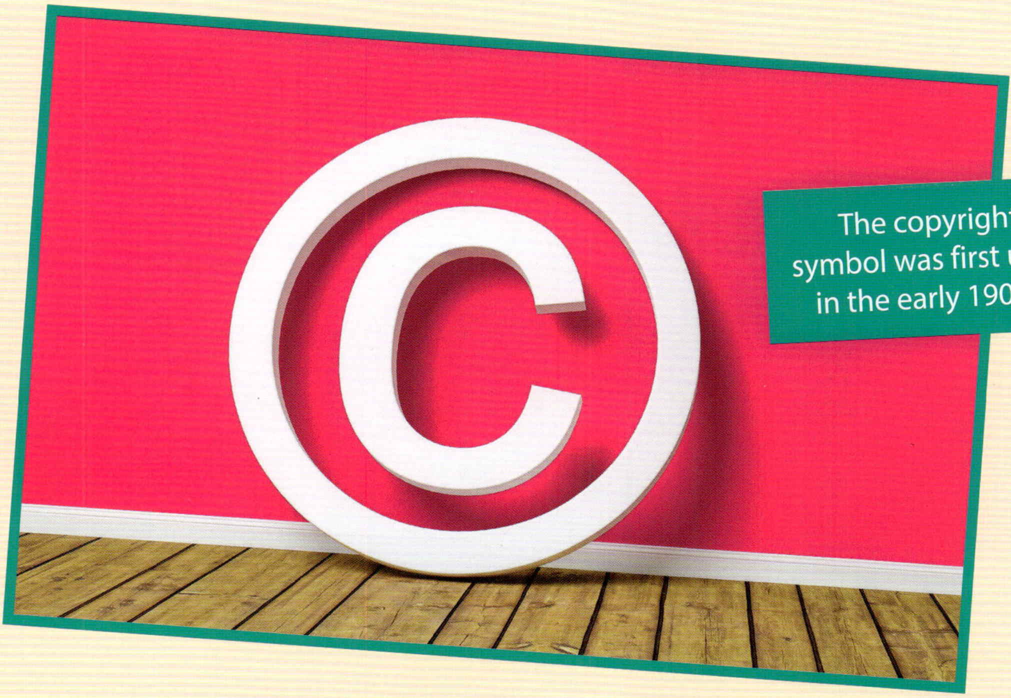

The copyright symbol was first used in the early 1900s.

Something does not seem right. Nate cannot borrow Mike's bike without asking. Why? It is Mike's property. Nate should ask for permission first. The same is true about using someone's ideas or intellectual property.

In the United States, copyright law protects the creative work of authors, designers, and artists. It states that people cannot use another person's work without the owner's permission. The copyright symbol is ©. This symbol tells you who owns intellectual property. Books include their copyright information on a page at the front or back. In this book, it is on page 24. You can find the same information on video games, CDs, DVDs, and other products.

Sometimes, intellectual property belongs to a group or a company. Game designer Jenny Smith works for a company called Video Fun. Video Fun makes and sells *Amazing Soccer*. Video Fun is the game's intellectual property owner. The copyright symbol appears with the company's name.

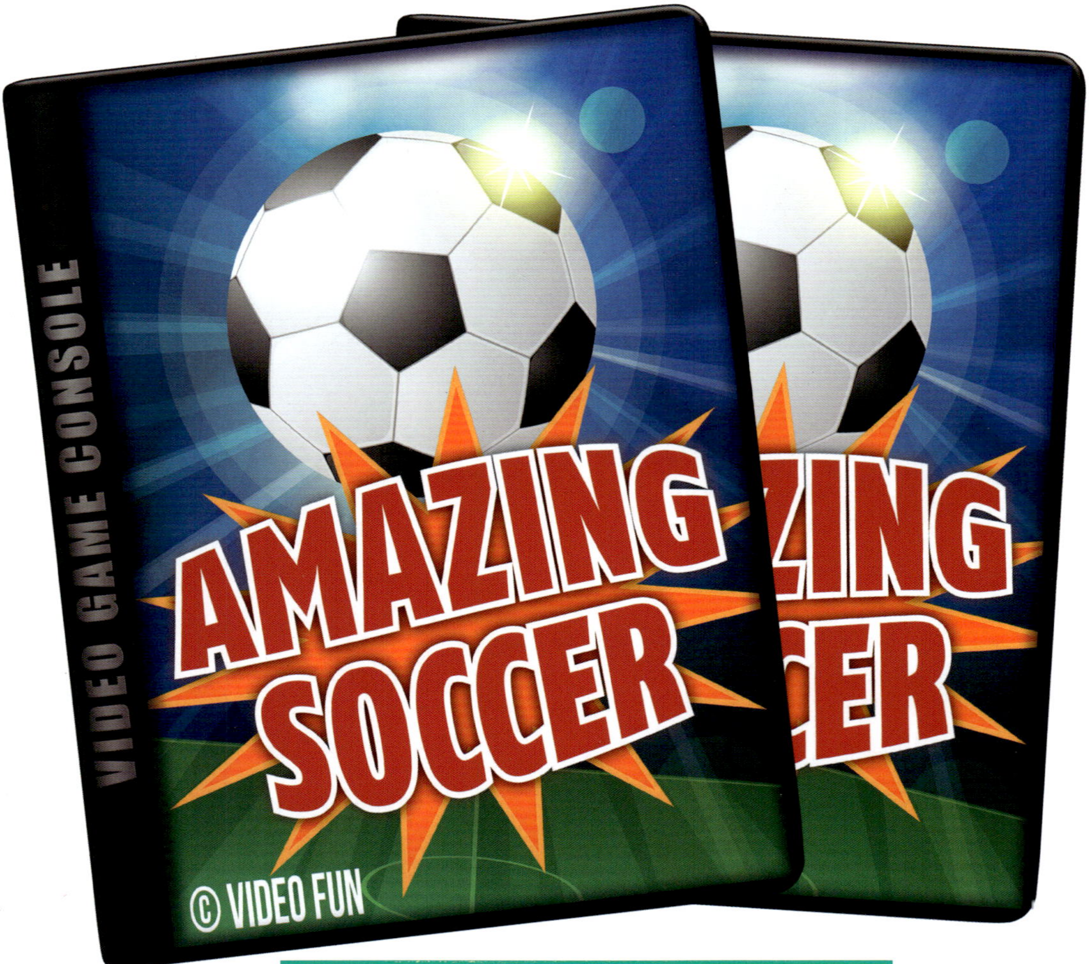

The copyright symbol appears by the name of the intellectual property owner.

Try This

Turn to page 24 in this book. Can you find the copyright symbol? What is the name of the publishing company that owns the copyright for this book? Other products have things similar to a book's copyright page. Pick up a video game or a DVD. Look for the copyright symbol. It is usually on the disc. You can also often find it on the case or box that came with it. Can you find who owns the intellectual property of each item?

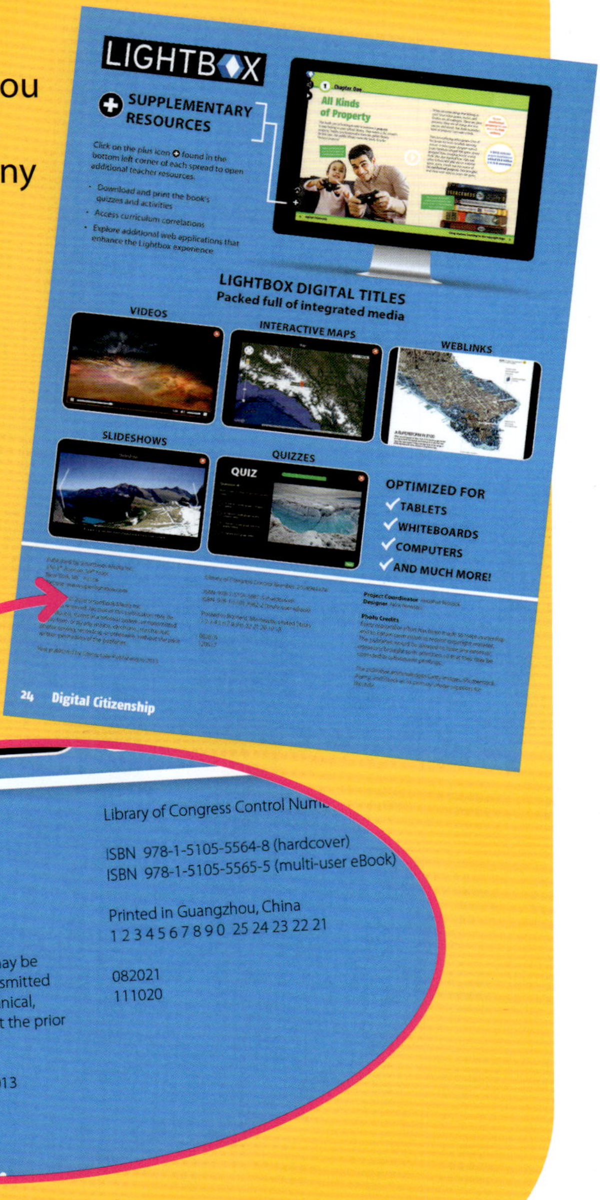

3 Chapter Three

Smart Steps to Using Information

Kids often use books and websites to find facts for school projects. They take notes to remember important ideas. Remember, the information in books and websites is someone's intellectual property. You need to be responsible about using these sources.

In 2015, about 60 percent of U.S. children had access to the internet at home.

Paraphrasing is a useful way to simplify information, such as when summarizing a story.

Follow these steps:

1. Read the book or website carefully. Try reading a few sentences or a paragraph at a time. Stop and ask yourself these questions:
   - What is the author's message?
   - How can I explain the idea in my own words without changing the meaning?

2. Write your notes in your own words. This is called **paraphrasing**. This is not just copying down phrases or sentences. Paraphrasing rewords ideas in a way that makes sense to you. It shows that you really understood what you read. Later, you can organize your facts in a way that is all your own.

The web address is sometimes called the uniform resource locator, or URL.

3. Write down the author's first and last names. Include the book or website's title, too. In a book, this information is on the copyright or title page. For a website, it is usually on the home page. Writing this down will help you credit your sources later.

4. Note the page number or web address where you found facts and ideas. The web address is found at the top of a web page. It usually starts with www. Some web addresses can be very long. In those cases, just record the address up to the first lone forward slash, or /.

Try This

Here is a page from a book called *All About Bats*. Can you paraphrase this information? Use a dictionary to help you understand any words you do not know.

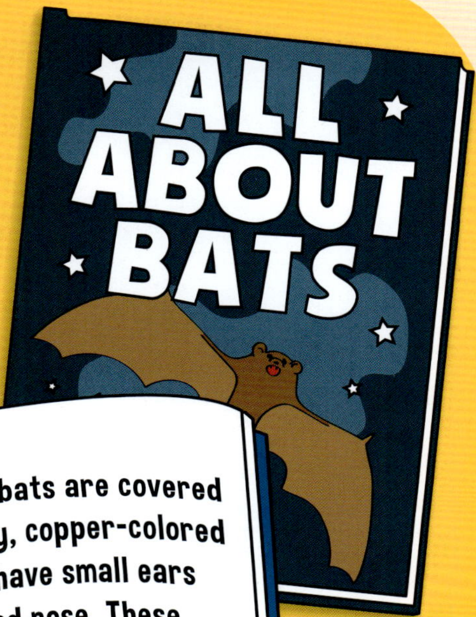

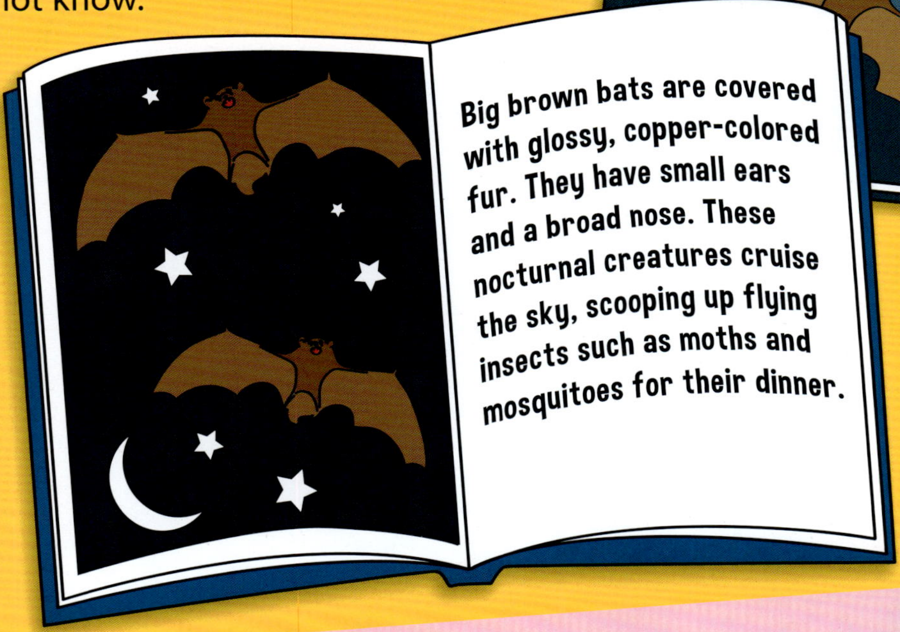
Big brown bats are covered with glossy, copper-colored fur. They have small ears and a broad nose. These nocturnal creatures cruise the sky, scooping up flying insects such as moths and mosquitoes for their dinner.

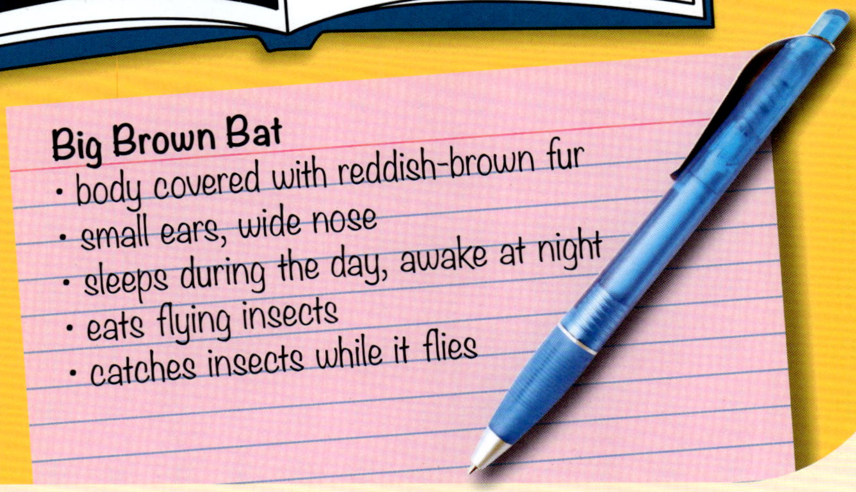
Big Brown Bat

- body covered with reddish-brown fur
- small ears, wide nose
- sleeps during the day, awake at night
- eats flying insects
- catches insects while it flies

4 Chapter Four

Giving Credit

You should always show where you found the information you used in a project. Do this by creating a **citation**. A citation is a list of facts that tell people about a book or website you have used.

Here is what you need to write a citation for a book:

1. Author's name
2. Title of the book
3. Page number(s) where you found facts or ideas. This is helpful if you or anyone reading your report wants to check your facts.

When you write a citation, separate the different parts using commas. Below is a citation for *All About Bats*.

James Shoe, All About Bats, p. 23

Do you need to write a citation for a website?
Here is what to include:

1. Author's name. This is often found at the bottom of the home page.
2. Website title. Not all websites have a title. If you cannot find one, skip this step.
3. Website URL
4. Date you viewed the website. The internet is constantly changing. It is a good idea to include this information in case the web page is changed or removed.

A website citation may look like this:

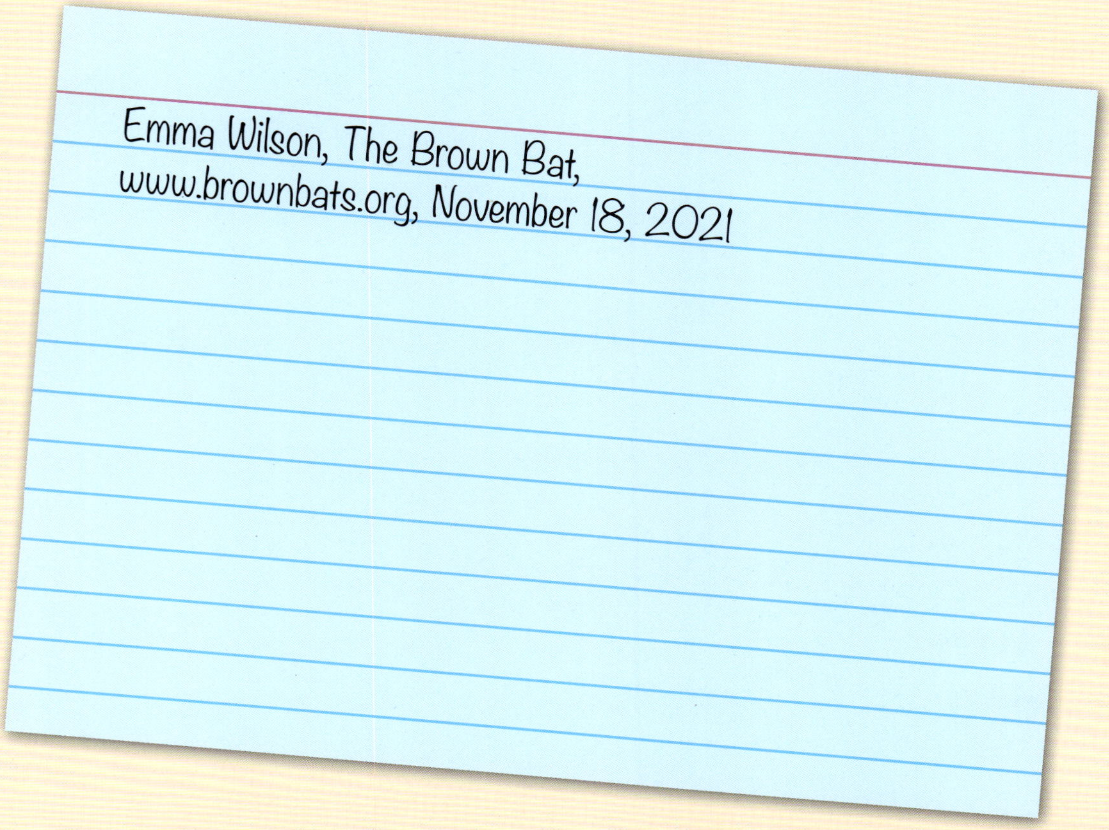

Information and ideas are all around us. They are in books, magazines, pictures, videos, and on the internet. Be a responsible user of information. Here is how:

- Use your own words to show what you understand.
- Use a citation to show where you found your information.
- Respect the intellectual property of others.

Many nonfiction books include credits for sources used by the author. These can help you find additional books to read on a topic.

Try This

Can you make citations for these sources?

Book
Title: *A Day at the Park*
Author: Peggy Wood
Page number: 17

Website
URL: www.shipatsea.net
Author: Edward West
Title: *Seeing Ships at Sea*
Date viewed: August 14, 2021

Quiz

1
What percentage of U.S. children had internet access at home in 2015?

2
When did the United States join the Berne Convention?

3
Can a video game be intellectual property?

4
When was the term intellectual property first used in the United States?

5
What is another name for a web address?

6
What is paraphrasing?

7
Where is the U.S. Copyright Office located?

8
How can someone show where they found the information they used in a project?

9
What does the word "intellect" relate to?

10
What does copyright law protect?

Answers: 1. About 60 percent **2.** 1988 **3.** Yes **4.** In the 19th century **5.** A URL **6.** Rewording ideas in a way that makes sense to you **7.** Washington, DC **8.** By creating a citation **9.** The human mind **10.** The creative work of authors, designers, and artists

Key Words

citation: a statement that shows where someone found information

copyright: the legal right to control the use of something created, such as a song or a book

intellect: the power of the mind to think, reason, understand, learn, and create

intellectual property: creative works that are legally protected by copyright, trademark, or patent

paraphrasing: saying or writing something in a different way than the original without changing the meaning

property: anything that is owned by an individual, group, or company

Index

authors 8, 11, 15, 16, 18, 19, 20, 21, 22

citations 18, 19, 20, 21, 22
company 5, 12, 13
copyright symbol 11, 12, 13

drawings 6
DVDs 11, 13

facts 14, 15, 16, 18

home page 16, 19

intellect 6, 22
intellectual property 4, 5, 6, 7, 11, 12, 13, 14, 20, 22

laws 8, 11, 22

notes 14, 15, 16

page number 16, 18, 21
paraphrasing 15, 17, 22

songs 6

title pages 16

uniform resource locator (URL) 16, 19, 21, 22

video games 4, 5, 11, 13, 22

LIGHTBOX

SUPPLEMENTARY RESOURCES

Click on the plus icon ⊕ found in the bottom left corner of each spread to open additional teacher resources.

- Download and print the book's quizzes and activities
- Access curriculum correlations
- Explore additional web applications that enhance the Lightbox experience

LIGHTBOX DIGITAL TITLES
Packed full of integrated media

VIDEOS

INTERACTIVE MAPS

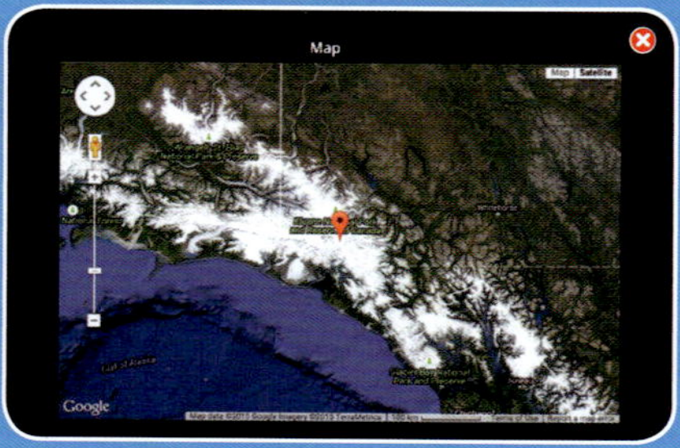

WEBLINKS

SLIDESHOWS

QUIZZES

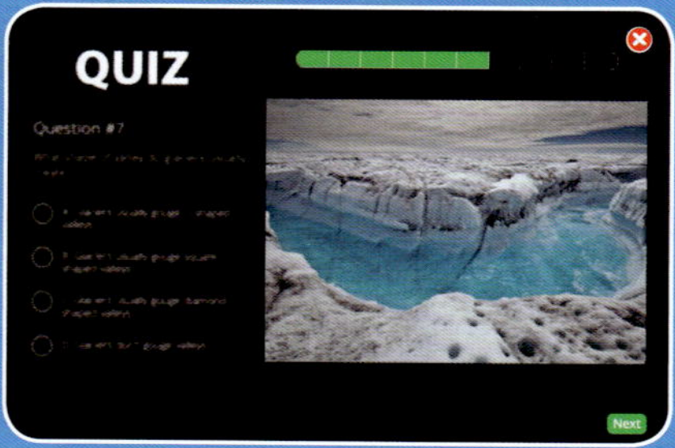

OPTIMIZED FOR

- ✓ TABLETS
- ✓ WHITEBOARDS
- ✓ COMPUTERS
- ✓ AND MUCH MORE!

Published by Lightbox Learning
276 5th Avenue
Suite 704 #917
New York, NY 10001
Website: www.openlightbox.com

Copyright ©2022 Lightbox Learning
All rights reserved. No part of this publication may be reproduced, stored in a retrieval system, or transmitted in any form or by any means, electronic, mechanical, photocopying, recording, or otherwise, without the prior written permission of the publisher.

First published by Cherry Lake Publishing in 2013

Library of Congress Control Number: 2021939447

ISBN 978-1-5105-5564-8 (hardcover)
ISBN 978-1-5105-5565-5 (multi-user eBook)

Printed in Guangzhou, China
1 2 3 4 5 6 7 8 9 0 25 24 23 22 21

082021
111020

Project Coordinator John Willis
Designer Jean Faye Marie Rodriguez

Photo Credits
Every reasonable effort has been made to trace ownership and to obtain permission to reprint copyright material. The publisher would be pleased to have any errors or omissions brought to its attention so that they may be corrected in subsequent printings.

The publisher acknowledges Getty Images and Shutterstock as its primary image suppliers for this title.